Halfway
to
Silence

Halfway to Silence

New Poems

By MAY SARTON

W. W. NORTON & COMPANY

NEW YORK · LONDON

Published simultaneously in Canada by George J. McLeod Limited,
Toronto. Printed in the United States of America.
All Rights Reserved

Library of Congress Cataloging in Publication Data
Sarton, May, 1912–
 Halfway to silence.

 Bibliography: p.
 Includes index.
 I. *Title.*
PS3537.A832H3   811'.5'2   79–24292
ISBN 0–393–01368–5
ISBN 0–393–00992–0 pbk.

2 3 4 5 6 7 8 9 0

Halfway to Silence

I was halfway to silence
Halfway to land's end
When I heard your voice.

Shall I take you with me?
Shall we go together
All the way to silence,
All the way to land's end?

Is there a choice?

Contents

Airs above the ground

I .

II

III

Some of these poems have appeared
in *Adam* (London), *Bennington Review*,
Choumia, *Christopher Street*, *Hardscuffle*,
Impact, *New York Quarterly*, *Virginia
Quarterly Review*, *Weid*, *Yankee*

Halfway
to
Silence

Airs Above the Ground

(Lippizan horse in Central Park)

The white horse floats above the field,
Pegasus in a child's dream by Chagall
Where gravity itself is forced to yield—
Oh marvelous beast who cannot ever fall!

The horse might have been sculpted flying there;
The muscles look engraved, taut flowing powers;
A furious gallop arrested in mid-air
Towers over the city's distant towers—

So wild and beautiful we have to laugh,
We have to weep. What is this caracole
That moves us with the strangeness of great art?
Dressage, control create a miracle.

Taught through the ages first to terrify,
To make foot soldiers turn their backs and scream
Before a stallion turned loose in the sky,
And now to bring us back to a lost dream—

What is released by concentrated hours,
The long dressage to catch a chancy rhyme,
And craft that may sometimes harness strange powers,
Those airs above the ground that banish time.

I

After All These Years

After all these years
When all I could caress
Was dog head and dog ears
When all that came to bless
Was cat with her loud purrs,
With what joy and what quake
I kiss small naked ears
And stroke a marble cheek,
After all these years
Let sleeping beauty wake.

Two Songs

1

Give me a love
That has never been,
Deeper than thought.
Bring earth alive,
The desert green
After long drought.

In the flesh, leaf,
In the bones, root,
The gardener's hand
Untangles grief,
Invents a land.

2

What other lover
Could ever displace
Despair with all-heal,
Or help me uncover
Sweet herb-of-grace
In the desolate field?
None had your face—
So pure in its poise,
So closed in its power,
That disciplined place
Where the tragic joys
Flower and re-flower.

The Oriole

When maples wear their aureole
Of gauzy green,
Then, only once, I heard the oriole
But rarely seen.

So it was when I found a home
After long unrest,
So it is once more now love has come
To hold me fast.

At the top of the great oak
As I said your name,
We saw him. He was there. He spoke.
The bird of flame.

Old Trees

Old trees—
How exquisite the white blossom
On the gnarled branch!
Thickened trunk, erratic shape
Battered by winter winds,
Bent in the long cold.

Young ones may please
The aesthete,
But old trees—
The miracle of their flowering
Against such odds—
Bring healing.

Let us praise them,
And sing hosannahs
As the small buds grow red
Just before they open.

A Voice

Blurred as though it has been woken
From an underground and secret river,
This voice itself and not the language spoken
Has made the air around me shiver.

Seductive sound, mysterious chord
That speaks its message in the very timbre
And not in a to be deciphered word
That I might hunt down or remember.

It wanders through my dreams and there I learn
I have to make the journey, have to go,
Whatever I must change or overturn
To reach the source, so strong this undertow.

Like a tapped glass the shivered air
Echoes and echoes a single poignant note.
That voice, where does it live? I must go there,
Comfort, entreat, and bless the magic throat.

The Balcony

after Baudelaire

Lover of silence, muse of the mysteries,
You will remember how we supped each night
There on your balcony high in the trees
Where a heraldic lion took late light,
Lover of silence, muse of the mysteries.

The big dogs slumbered near us like good bears;
The old cat begged a morsel from my plate,
And all around leaves stirred in the warm airs
Breathed from the valley as the red sun set.
The big dogs slumbered near us like good bears.

I thought of all the pain and how we met
Late in our lives yet lavishly at ease,
Having assumed an end to old regret
In the eternal present of the trees—
I thought of all the pain and how we met.

There every night we drank deep of the wine
And of our love, still without history,
Yet the completion of some real design
Earned with much thought, muse of the mystery.
There every night we drank deep of the wine.

While out of deprivation a huge flower,
The evening's passion, was about to bloom.
Such intimacy held us in its power
The long years vanished in a little room,
And out of deprivation, a huge flower.

The Myths Return

Now in this armature
Where the tide rose and rose
Till every crack was filled,
Long echoes still
Reverberate in the hollow cave,
And the walls tremble.

Poseidon
Catching a dolphin
Must have laughed in his fierce joy.
Eons ago
Sacred and creaturely married,
And still those great tides ebb and flow—

As we now know.

Time for Rich Silence

Time for rich silence,
The passionate season,
For the present tense
Beyond speech, outside reason.

Time now to explore
These intricate cages,
Two bodies aware,
Two equipages.

Find the way to unlock
A mysterious door
At the threshold of shock
With the impact of war.

Then gentle fierce joys
On the wave's rising curve
Till it reaches it poise,
Tumbles, touches the nerve.

And all tumult is done—
Two equipages
In silent communion
Released from their cages.

Three Things

I carried two things around in my mind
Walking the woods and thinking how to say
Shiver of poplar leaves in a light wind,
Threshing of water over tumbled stones,
A brook rippling its interrupted way—
Two things that bring a tremor to the bones.

And now I carry around in my head a third.
The force of it stops me as I walk the wood,
Three things for which no one has found a word—
Wind in the poplar, tremor under the skin
Deep in the flesh, a shiver of more than blood
When lovers, water, and leaves are wholly one.

The Lady of the Lake

Somewhere at the bottom of the lake she is
Entangled among weeds, her deep self drowned.
I cannot be with her there. I know she is bound
To a dead man. Her wide open eyes are his.
Only a part of her surfaces in my arms
When I can lift her up and float her there
Gently to breathe life-giving natural air,
Wind in the leaves, the bright summer's charms.

For I know I can be hers, hers for a while
But she can never be mine for a year or a day,
Long ago married, her deep self given away,
Though she turns to me sometimes with a luminous smile.
But what I cannot have or cannot keep
Draws me down under the waters, and I come
With him, with her, into a strange communion,
And all is well where the drowned lovers sleep.

First Autumn

What do the trees in the window have to tell
The lovers wrapped in their strange grief,
The lovers wrapped in their strange delight?
What do they hear in the rain, caught in its spell?
What do they see in the turning of a leaf?
What more to be told before the coming of night?

These two who are far apart and yet so near,
These two together and so much alone
Like stars set somewhere out in darkest space—
The trees may say they have nothing to fear.
The rain may tell of wearing down a stone,
But the moody lovers tremble before a face.

The trees in the window are turning toward sleep,
Their light a changing light at the year's turning,
And the rain repeats its lonely plaintive phrase.
How can these fragile lovers hope to keep
A crimson leaf from falling, or this burning
Maintain forever some hint of their great days?

Mal du Départ

After you have gone
I walk up and down
The strange chilling tomb
This lively house has suddenly become.

Even your white tulips
Turn brown at the lips,
Their freshness gone,
And ashes on the hearth. I am alone.

Absence infects the air
And it is everywhere.
How can I shake off woe,
On what bed lay me down without you?

What healing sacrament
What ritual invent
And quietly perform
To bring life back and make it warm?

Another day a letter
Might tell you I am better,
The invalid has taken
Some food, is less forlorn and shaken.

But for today it's true
That I can hardly draw
A solitary breath
That does not hurt me like a little death.

II

Jealousy

When I was a child
I walked a forest floor
Charred black after the great trees burned.
The air was acrid.
Among old roots the fire still crept.
Sometimes a small blue flame
Licked at the soles of my feet,
While overhead
Birds hunted their nests.

Fifty years ago
I saw what it means to burn.
I met the destructive flame,
But only now I am old
Have I come to know
Its name.

Control

Hold the tiger fast in check
Put the leash around his neck.
Make it known a growl will tighten
The collar. Browbeat. Frighten.

Set the tiger on a tightrope.
Make him walk it, make him cope.
Punish any slightest fumble.
Make him walk it. Watch him tremble.

Yours the power to use or not
Once the fierce soul has been caught.
Yours to beat without forgiveness
What is wild with fear and loss.

You may have complete control.
There will be no roar or growl.
But can you look into those eyes
Where the smothered fire lies?

Tame the tiger. Break his pride.
You will find yourself outside
With all those who can destroy
Tiger love and tiger joy.

Outside in the awful dark,
Smothered every smallest spark
Where nothing blesses or can bless,
How will you bear the loneliness?

Along a Brook

Water over sand,
I did not take your hand.
Water over stone,
We were each alone,

In the green keep
Of the wood we walked
As though half asleep.
Only birds talked.

Only dogs played
Among rock and root
In the dappled shade
And moss underfoot.

In the grave place
Could not take your hand.
I had lost my face.
Water over sand.

Water over stone.
How far did I go
Through the thick pain
Into darker shadow?

But I found my face
When I looked at you
In the grave place—
When I could look through

To the stubborn child
Who cannot be wrong,
And forgave the child,
And could sing my song.

Beggar, Queen, and Ghost

I have been a beggar with a begging bowl.
I have been a queen with a golden crown.
I have been so hungry I ate my soul,
But never outcast and never thrown down
Since I was alive
And able to give.

But never the beggar and never the queen
Could live without hope behind a closed door,
And the hungry poor never felt this pain,
In the place where I could not give of my store,
Not a crown of glory
Nor a beggar's story.

There the beggar laid down his bowl and cried.
There the queen took off her golden crown.
There the woman who ate her soul nearly died.
There buried so deep all praise and renown
That the lonely guest
Had become a ghost.

And there I learned that hell is the place
Where I cannot give (like a barren wife?)
Where the soul is locked in behind a face,
Where none of my riches can flow into life,
Devalued, outcast,
Queen, beggar, and ghost.

The Country of Pain

In the country of pain we are each alone.
Only joy brings communion, the light game
When passion tosses the ball high in air
And we forget Medusa who turns love to stone,
And Circe who knows every pig by name,
And manic-depressive Eros in despair.

In the country of pain there is no defence.
Tears scandalize. If we try to get through
To some rock of truth we are chastised
Like children whose anguish may be immense,
And told not to make scenes when all we know
Is terrible loss and true love ill-used.

In the country of pain we are animals
Who cannot understand a sudden blow
Or trust in a redeemer. There is none.
For pain is the country of lost souls
Which the gods flee because they know
They cannot re-humanize the pig or stone.

What redeemer now could return lost joys
Imprisoned by an ethos, beaten down,
The things made cheap within a damaged psyche,
The mysterious, magical, fantastic toys
Love showers on us with beautiful abandon
When manic-depressive Eros has a high?

For always what looked like an easy game
Becomes too frightening for innocence to play.
The country of Eros becomes the country of pain,
And the beglamored pigs who gladly came
To Circe's call die in some horrible way
As Medusa begins her cold cruel reign.

Out of Touch

The source is silted
That flowed so fast and clear
Packed down, polluted,
The goddess in despair.

The dry mouth burns
In this infernal drought.
The goddess flees and turns
Not to be caught.

Animal pride is broken.
Children are murderers,
The deprived overtaken
By strange disorders.

The goddess turns away
From cages like these.
Hers love's fierce joy and play
Not its bleak miseries.

At the Black Rock

Anger's the beast in me.
In you it is pride.
When they meet they lock.
There is no pity.
At the black rock
Where the beasts hide

Love turns to hate
In a cruel war,
And once it's begun
It is always too late
To be patient or fair.
And no one can win.

Let us go to the rock
Where the beasts hide
And kneeling there, pray
For some heart-cracking shock
To set us both free
From anger and pride.

At the cold impasse
Tame the anguished cries,
Mend what has been torn,
Bring the animals peace
Where they stand forlorn
With love in their eyes.

Can I do it? Can you?
It means yielding all.
It means going naked
No refuge but rue,
Admitting stark need—
Eden after the fall.

III

The Turning of the Wind

Love waits for a turning of the wind.
Elusive, patient, every early morning,
Although the humid heat has not been kind,
Love waits for clear air, an end to mourning.

There is a wall. What wind to blow it down?
What power cleanse the awful fetid air
And burn the haze away, what brilliant sun
To show us the rich landscape is still there?

We cannot hear each other. Truth gets lost.
Lack of rapport has damaged the whole range
Of what we might redeem that pain has cost.
So love waits for the wind to change.

After the Storm

The roar of big surf and above it all night
The peepers singing out so sweet and frail!
Above the pounding roar that wears down rock
They dare, they try to connect through the gale.
And if that relentless boom might seem to mock
Those who still risk their hope before daylight,
That song suggests something is going right.
Whatever locked love cannot bear to do,
The tree frogs can, and spring is breaking through.

Love

Fragile as a spider's web
Hanging in space
Between tall grasses,
It is torn again and again.
A passing dog
Or simply the wind can do it.
Several times a day
I gather myself together
And spin it again.

Spiders are patient weavers.
They never give up.
And who knows
What keeps them at it?
Hunger, no doubt,
And hope.

Of Molluscs

As the tide rises, the closed mollusc
Opens a fraction to the ocean's food,
Bathed in its riches. Do not ask
What force would do, or if force could.

A knife is of no use against a fortress.
You might break it to pieces as gulls do.
No, only the rising tide and its slow progress
Opens the shell. Lovers, I tell you true.

You who have held yourselves closed hard
Against warm sun and wind, shelled up in fears
And hostile to a touch or tender word—
The ocean rises, salt as unshed tears.

Now you are floated on this gentle flood
That cannot force or be forced, welcome food
Salt as your tears, the rich ocean's blood,
Eat, rest, be nourished on the tide of love.

June Wind

I watched wind ripple the field's supple grasses.
For once earth is alive while restless ocean
Lies still beyond it like a flat blue screen.
I watch the wind burnishing as it passes,
Lifting soft waves, an ecstasy of motion,
A long glissando through the static green.

These waves crash on no rock; rooted, they stay,
As restless love, that ocean, changes over
And comes to land, alive, a shining field
Caught in wind's captivating gentle play
As though a harp played by a subtle lover—
And the tormented ocean has been stilled.

The Summer Tree

In all the summer glut of green,
Serrated leaves, a dark and shifty screen,

Catalpa flowers, unseasonal surprise,
To tense the landscape up for drowsy eyes.

We come alive beholding points of white,
Among the leaves, immense rosettes alight.

The blessing of pure form that opens space
And makes us stop and look in sudden peace.

Late Autumn

On random wires the rows of summer swallows
Wait for their lift-off. They will soon be gone
Before All Saints and before All Hallows,
The changing time when we are most alone.

Disarmed, too vulnerable, full of dread,
And once again as naked as the trees
Before the dark, precarious days ahead,
And troubled skies over tumultuous seas.

When we are so transparent to the dead
There is no wall. We hear their voices speak,
And as the small birds wheel off overhead
We bend toward the earth suddenly weak.

How to believe that all will not be lost?
Our flowers, too, not perish in the blight?
Love, leave me your South against the frost.
Say "hush" to my fears, and warm the night.

The Geese

The geese honked overhead.
I ran to catch the skein
To watch them as they fled
In a long wavering line.

I caught my breath, alone,
Abandoned like a lover
With winter at the bone
To see the geese go over.

It happens every year
And every year some woman
Haunted by loss and fear
Must take it as an omen,

Must shiver as she stands
Watching the wild geese go,
With sudden empty hands
Before the cruel snow.

Some woman every year
Must catch her breath and weep
With so much wildness near
At all she cannot keep.

Autumn Sonnets

How can we name it "fall," this slow ascent
From dawn to dawn, each purer than the last,
As structure comes back through the golden tent
And shimmering color floats down to be lost?
How can we name it "fall," this elevation
As all our earthly shelter drops away
And we stand poised as if for revelation
On the brink of another startling day,
And still must live with ever greater height,
And skies more huge and luminous at dusk,
Till we are strained by light and still more light
As if this progress were an imposed task
Demanding of love supreme clarity,
Impersonal, stark as the winter sky.

Everywhere, in my garden, in my thought
I batten down, shore up, and prune severely.
All tender plants are cut down to the root.
My gentle earth is barren now, or nearly.
Harden it well against the loss and change;
Prepare to hold the fastness, since I know
This open self must grow more harsh and strange
Before it meets the softness of the snow.
Withstand, endure, the worst is still to come.
Wild animals seek shelter from the cold,
But I am as exposed here safe at home
As the wild fox running outside the fold:
He burns his brightness for mere food or bed.
I contain love as if it were a warhead.

Pruning the Orchard

Out there in the orchard they have come
To prune the overgrowth, cut back and free
The crisscrossed branches of apple and plum,
Shaping the formless back to symmetry.

They do not work for beauty's sake
But to improve the harvest come next year.
Each tough lopsided branch they choose to break
Is broken toward fruit more crisp and rare.

I watch them, full of wonder and dismay,
Feeling the need to shape my life, be calm,
Like the untroubled pruners who, all day,
Cut back, are ruthless, and without a qualm.

While I, beleaguered, always conscience-torn,
Have let the thickets stifle peaceful growth,
Spontaneous flow stopped, poems stillborn,
Imagined duties, pebbles in my mouth.

Muse, pour strength into my pruning wrist
That I may cut the way toward open space,
A timeless orchard, poetry-possessed,
There without guilt to contemplate your face.

Old Lovers at the Ballet

In the dark theatre lovers sit
Watching the supple dancers weave
A fugue, motion and music melded.
There on the stage below, brilliantly lit
No dancer stumbles or may grieve;
Their very smiles are disciplined and moulded.

And in the dark old lovers feel dismay
Watching the ardent bodies leap and freeze,
Thinking how age has changed them and has mocked.
Once they were light and bold in lissome play,
Limber as willows that could bend with ease—
But as they watch a vision is unlocked.

Imagination springs the trap of youth.
And in the dark motionless, as they stare,
Old lovers reach new wonders and new answers
As in the mind they leap to catch the truth,
For young the soul was awkward, unaware,
That claps its hands now with the supple dancers.

And in the flesh those dancers cannot spare
What the old lovers have had time to learn,
That the soul is a lithe and serene athlete
That deepens touch upon the darkening air.
It is not energy but light they burn,
The radiant powers of the Paraclete.

IV

On Sark

The isle is for islanders, some born—
They like being surrounded by
And anchored in the ever-changing sea,
For it is just this being enclosed
In a small space within a huge space
That makes them feel both safe and free,
Tilling small fields under a huge sky.

The isle is for islanders, some made—
They are drawn here, the two-in-one,
To be alone together, hand in hand,
Walking the silence of the high plateau
Where bees and heather marry well,
Or down long flights of stairs to caves.
Love is the summer island, safe and wild.

Islands are for people who are islands,
Who have always been detached from the main
For a purpose, or because they crave
The free within the framed as poets do,
The solitary for whom being alone
Is not a loneliness but fertile good.
Here on this island I feel myself at home.

And because I am here, happy among the bees,
A donkey in the field, the crooked paths
That lead me always to some precipitous fall
And the sudden opening out of blue below,
Hope flows back into my crannies now.
I am ready to begin the long journey
Toward love, the mainland, perhaps not alone.

In Suffolk

Mourning my old ways, guilt fills the mind,
As memories well up from ripening gold
And I look far away over tilted land
Watching splashed light and shadow on the fold
Where restless clouds flock over and disband.
To what have I been faithful in the end?

What lover loved forever well or ill?
As clouds come over to darken a line of trees
And then far off shadow a wooded hill,
I have to answer, "faithful only to these,
To earth itself turning toward the fall,
To earth's relentless changing mysteries."

All lovers sow and reap their harvests from
This flesh ever to be renewed and reconceived
As the bright ploughs break open the dark loam.
Whatever the cost and whatever I believed,
Only the earth itself, great honeycomb,
Gives comfort to the many times bereaved.

Whatever cloud comes over with black rain
To make my life seem of so little worth,
To cover the bright gold with guilt and pain,
The poem, life itself, labor of birth
Has been forced back again and again
To find renewal in the fertile earth.

Fidelity to what? To a gnarled tree, a root,
To the necessity for growth and discipline.
Now I am old why mourn what had to go?
Despite the loss and so much fallen fruit,
The harvest is so rich it fills my bin.
What had to grow has been allowed to grow.

A Winter Notebook

1

Low tide—
The sea's slow motion,
The surge and slur
Over rocky shingle.

A few gulls ride
Rocking-horse waves.

Under blurred gray sky
The field shines white.

2

I am not available
At the moment
Except to myself.

Downstairs the plumber
Is emptying the big tank,
Water-logged.
The pump pumped on and on
And might have worn out.

So many lives pour into this house,
Sometimes I get too full;
The pump wears out.

So now I am emptying the tank.
It is not an illness
That keeps me from writing.
I am simply staying alive
As one does
At times by taking in,
At times by shutting out.

3

I wake in a wide room
Before dawn,
Just a little light framed by three windows.

I wake in a large space
Listening to the gentle hush of waves.

I watch the sea open like a flower
A huge blue flower
As the sun rises
Out of the dark.

4

It is dark when I go downstairs
And always the same shiver
As I turn on the light—
There they are, alive in the cold,
Hyacinths, begonias,
Cyclamen, a cloud of bloom
As though they were birds
Settled for a moment in the big window.

I wake my hand, still half asleep,
With a sweet geranium leaf.

After breakfast
I tend to all their needs,
These extravagant joys,
Become a little drunk on green
And the smell of earth.

We have lived through another
Bitter cold night.

5

On this dark cold morning
After the ice storm
A male pheasant
Steps precisely across the snow.

His red and gold,
The warmth and shine of him
In the white freeze,
Explosive!
A firecracker pheasant
Opens the new year.

6

I sit at my desk under attack,
Trying to survive
Panic and guilt, the flu . . .

Outside
Even sunlight looks cold
Glancing off glare ice.

Inside,
Narcissus in bloom,
And a patch of sun on the pile
Of unanswered letters.

I lift my eyes
To the blue
Open-ended ocean.
Why worry?
Some things are always there.

7

The ornamental cherry
Is alive
With cedar waxwings,
Their dandy crests silhouetted
Against gray sky.

They are after cherries,
Dark-red jewels
In frozen clusters
On the asymmetrical twigs.

In the waste of dirty snow
The scene is as brilliant
As a Rajput painting.

I note the yellow-banded tail feathers,
A vermilion accent on the wing—
What elegance!

8

The dark islands
Float on a silvery sea.

I see them like a mirage
Through the branches of the great oak.
After the leaves come out
They will be gone—
These winter joys

And snow coming tonight.

Of the Muse

There is no poetry in lies,
But in crude honesty
There is hope for poetry.
For a long time now
I have been deprived of it
Because of pride,
Would not allow myself
The impossible.
Today, I have learned
That to become
A great, cracked,
Wide-open door
Into nowhere
Is wisdom.

When I was young,
I misunderstood
The Muse.
Now I am older and wiser,
I can be glad of her
As one is glad of the light.
We do not thank the light,
But rejoice in what we see
Because of it.
What I see today
Is the snow falling:
All things are made new.

Index